This book belongs to:

_____

Wishing you:

Best of Luck
From:

Wishing you:

Best of Luck
From:

Wishing you:

Best of Luck
From:

Wishing you:

Best of Luck
From:

Wishing you:

Best of Luck
From:

Wishing you:

Best of Luck
From:

Wishing you:

Best of Luck
From:

Wishing you:

Best of Luck
From:

Wishing you:

Best of Luck
From:

Wishing you:

Best of Luck
From:

Wishing you:

Best of Luck
From:

Wishing you:

Best of Luck
From:

Wishing you:

Best of Luck
From:

Wishing you:

Best of Luck
From:

Wishing you:

Best of Luck
From:

Wishing you:

Best of Luck
From:

Wishing you:

Best of Luck
From:

Wishing you:

Best of Luck
From:

Wishing you:

Best of Luck
From:

Wishing you:

Best of Luck
From:

Wishing you:

Best of Luck
From:

Wishing you:

Best of Luck
From:

Wishing you:

Best of Luck
From:

Wishing you:

Best of Luck
From:

Wishing you:

Best of Luck
From:

Wishing you:

Best of Luck
From:

Wishing you: Best of Luck
                                From:

Wishing you: Best of Luck
                                From:

Wishing you:

Best of Luck
From:

Wishing you:

Best of Luck
From:

Wishing you: Best of Luck
                      From:

Wishing you: Best of Luck
                      From:

Wishing you:

Best of Luck
From:

Wishing you:

Best of Luck
From:

Wishing you:

Best of Luck
From:

Wishing you:

Best of Luck
From:

Wishing you:

Best of Luck
From:

Wishing you:

Best of Luck
From:

Wishing you:

Best of Luck
From:

Wishing you:

Best of Luck
From:

Wishing you:

Best of Luck
From:

Wishing you:

Best of Luck
From:

Wishing you:

Best of Luck
From:

Wishing you:

Best of Luck
From:

Wishing you:

Best of Luck
From:

Wishing you:

Best of Luck
From:

Wishing you:

Best of Luck
From:

Wishing you:

Best of Luck
From:

Wishing you:

Best of Luck
From:

Wishing you:

Best of Luck
From:

Wishing you:

Best of Luck
From:

Wishing you:

Best of Luck
From:

Wishing you:

Best of Luck
From:

Wishing you:

Best of Luck
From:

Wishing you:

Best of Luck
From:

Wishing you:

Best of Luck
From:

Wishing you:

Best of Luck
From:

Wishing you:

Best of Luck
From:

Wishing you:

Best of Luck
From:

Wishing you:

Best of Luck
From:

Wishing you:

Best of Luck
From:

Wishing you:

Best of Luck
From:

Wishing you:

Best of Luck
From:

Wishing you:

Best of Luck
From:

Wishing you:

Best of Luck
From:

Wishing you:

Best of Luck
From:

Wishing you:

Best of Luck
From:

Wishing you:

Best of Luck
From:

Wishing you:

Best of Luck
From:

Wishing you:

Best of Luck
From:

Wishing you:

Best of Luck
From:

Wishing you:

Best of Luck
From:

Wishing you:

Best of Luck
From:

Wishing you:

Best of Luck
From:

Wishing you:

Best of Luck
From:

Wishing you:

Best of Luck
From:

Wishing you:

Best of Luck
From:

Wishing you:

Best of Luck
From:

Wishing you:

Best of Luck
From:

Wishing you:

Best of Luck
From:

Wishing you:

Best of Luck
From:

Wishing you:

Best of Luck
From:

Wishing you:

Best of Luck
From:

Wishing you:

Best of Luck
From:

Wishing you:

Best of Luck
From:

Wishing you:

Best of Luck
From:

Wishing you: Best of Luck
                                From:

Wishing you: Best of Luck
                                From:

Wishing you:

Best of Luck
From:

Wishing you:

Best of Luck
From:

Wishing you:

Best of Luck
From:

Wishing you:

Best of Luck
From:

Wishing you:

Best of Luck
From:

Wishing you:

Best of Luck
From:

Wishing you:

Best of Luck
From:

Wishing you:

Best of Luck
From:

Wishing you:

Best of Luck
From:

Wishing you:

Best of Luck
From:

Wishing you:

Best of Luck
From:

Wishing you:

Best of Luck
From:

Wishing you: Best of Luck
                                From:

Wishing you: Best of Luck
                                From:

Wishing you: Best of Luck
From:

Wishing you: Best of Luck
From:

Wishing you:

Best of Luck
From:

Wishing you:

Best of Luck
From:

Wishing you: Best of Luck
                                From:

Wishing you: Best of Luck
                                From:

Wishing you:

Best of Luck
From:

Wishing you:

Best of Luck
From:

Wishing you:

Best of Luck
From:

Wishing you:

Best of Luck
From:

Wishing you:

Best of Luck
From:

Wishing you:

Best of Luck
From:

Wishing you:

Best of Luck
From:

Wishing you:

Best of Luck
From:

Wishing you:

Best of Luck
From:

Wishing you:

Best of Luck
From:

Wishing you:

Best of Luck
From:

Wishing you:

Best of Luck
From:

Wishing you:

Best of Luck
From:

Wishing you:

Best of Luck
From:

Wishing you:

Best of Luck
From:

Wishing you:

Best of Luck
From:

Wishing you:

Best of Luck
From:

Wishing you:

Best of Luck
From:

Wishing you:

Best of Luck
From:

Wishing you:

Best of Luck
From:

Wishing you:

Best of Luck
From:

Wishing you:

Best of Luck
From:

Wishing you:

Best of Luck
From:

Wishing you:

Best of Luck
From:

Wishing you:

Best of Luck
From:

Wishing you:

Best of Luck
From:

Wishing you:

Best of Luck
From:

Wishing you:

Best of Luck
From:

Wishing you:

Best of Luck
From:

Wishing you:

Best of Luck
From:

Wishing you:

Best of Luck
From:

Wishing you:

Best of Luck
From:

Wishing you:

Best of Luck
From:

Wishing you:

Best of Luck
From:

Wishing you:

Best of Luck
From:

Wishing you:

Best of Luck
From:

Wishing you:

Best of Luck
From:

Wishing you:

Best of Luck
From:

Wishing you:

Best of Luck
From:

Wishing you:

Best of Luck
From:

Wishing you:

Best of Luck
From:

Wishing you:

Best of Luck
From:

Wishing you:

Best of Luck
From:

Wishing you:

Best of Luck
From:

Wishing you:

Best of Luck
From:

Wishing you:

Best of Luck
From:

Wishing you:

Best of Luck
From:

Wishing you:

Best of Luck
From:

Wishing you:

Best of Luck
From:

Wishing you:

Best of Luck
From:

Wishing you:

Best of Luck
From:

Wishing you:

Best of Luck
From:

Wishing you:

Best of Luck
From:

Wishing you:

Best of Luck
From:

Wishing you:

Best of Luck
From:

Wishing you:

Best of Luck
From:

Wishing you:

Best of Luck
From:

Wishing you:

Best of Luck
From:

Wishing you:

Best of Luck
From:

Wishing you:

Best of Luck
From:

Wishing you:

Best of Luck
From:

Wishing you:

Best of Luck
From:

Wishing you:

Best of Luck
From:

Wishing you:

Best of Luck
From:

Wishing you:

Best of Luck
From:

Wishing you:

Best of Luck
From:

Wishing you:

Best of Luck
From:

Wishing you:

Best of Luck
From:

Wishing you:

Best of Luck
From:

Wishing you:

Best of Luck
From:

Wishing you:

Best of Luck
From:

Wishing you:

Best of Luck
From:

Wishing you:

Best of Luck
From:

Wishing you:

Best of Luck
From:

Wishing you:

Best of Luck
From:

Wishing you:

Best of Luck
From:

Wishing you:

Best of Luck
From:

Wishing you:

Best of Luck
From:

Wishing you:

Best of Luck
From:

Wishing you:

Best of Luck
From:

Wishing you:

Best of Luck
From:

Wishing you:

Best of Luck
From:

Wishing you:

Best of Luck
From:

Wishing you:

Best of Luck
From:

Gift	Received from

Gift	Received from

Made in the USA
Monee, IL
12 May 2022

96280189R00057